About the Author

Jessica Belyea has been a successful reseller for over a year. She provides stylish, comfortable clothing to women in her city where size-inclusive shopping is limited, from both her home and - to a lesser extent - a local market. Her background in personal training and management has given her a broad base in sales, client service, and goal setting skills that are transferred across many venues. She used her skill in sales to sell clothing in a capacity that she was able to quit her day job, allowing her to sell and write full-time. She enjoys the opportunity to service a clientele looking for convenient, affordable shopping.

Intro

These days, many people are looking for alternative income streams to support their homes and families, allow for leisure activities, and to squirrel away a nest egg. Perhaps you want a steady side-gig to earn income additional to your current wage, or maybe you dream of quitting your current job and working for yourself full-time.

Reselling is one of the easiest ways to earn supplemental income. You decide on your niche(s), shop for and purchase items at a good price, then sell them for a profit. Your options on what you want to sell are limitless, and you can work on a scope as large or modest as you wish

While there are notable benefits with this plan, there are - as with all business ventures - pitfalls and challenges as well. That's where this book comes in.

This is not your average how-to. This is a compendium of my experiences in reselling designed to help you to achieve success and mitigate failure. I put in a lot of work in trialing different systems to be a prosperous reseller, and I have compiled all of my best advice here for you.

The book is not a rigid, unforgiving series of steps. Rather, it is an adaptable protocol to allow your skills, preferences, and personality to shine through. When you follow my advice and use all of the tools listed, you will become an unstoppable reselling machine. You will become focused and resilient, and able to utilize exceptional sales techniques that will help you to earn fringe income.

One of the best things about reselling is that you can work in whatever arena best suits your current knowledge and access. I chose women's clothing because I know - from my experience in sales - that a 30-50 year old female demographic works extremely well for me.

What products do you love? It is easy to speak on them, and to know what is of good (and poor) quality, what the general pricing is, trends and staples in that area, etc. This base knowledge will give you the confidence to sell.

When I dove into this business I had no experience and no direction. All I knew was that I wanted to make enough money reselling that I could support my family while I wrote and cooked full-time. I applied my background in sales, an organizational system and quickly developed a proficiency to allow me to do exactly what I wanted.

So if you are ready to earn some money, learn my secret weapon best practices, and avoid common pitfalls that other resellers make, let's get started.
Thank you for trusting me to help get you started through this journey. Stay focused, reference back as much as needed and I feel confident that you will make wondrous, profitable change in your life. I wish you all the best!

Jessica

1. Start with you. Why do you want to head into resale as a way to earn income? How much money do you need to

make? What skills do you have that will help you? What skills do you need to work on?

The more you know about how this will actually impact you as you begin the journey, the easier it is to stay focused, avoid getting stuck, and actually even enjoy it!

There are many aspects of resale that are positive, and some that are negative, so you need to weigh it out against your day to make sure it is right for you.

2.	Put the hours in. In this business, you get out what you put in. It really does pay to take
the time to establish an organization system, take decent photos, check your listings for typos, and respond timely to customers.

Imagine you are paying an employee for your own business. How much would you pay them for 20 minutes of work? Now, how much would you pay them for 5 hours of work? Is it different? Of course! So don't expect to make money without investing some time.

Of course this is going to be different for everybody, depending on what other obligations you have in your life. But it is worth tracking how much time you are spending when it comes time to evaluate yourself on your success.

3.	What arena do you want to sell in? Will you be selling in a store or market? Using a
local online program such as Kijiji, Craigslist, or Facebook Marketplace? Are you willing to ship worldwide and use a large retailer like eBay? Perhaps a combination?

Although there are certainly a lot of similarities between these avenues, there are also important differences to take into account.

Being in a market setting means you get face-to-face time with customers, but it also means you have to devote that time.

Selling online means taking time to write out descriptions and take photos, but allows you to do other work during downtime.

Selling across country or internationally means you have a much larger group of potential customers, but you need to take packing and shipping logistics and costs into account.

4.   Once you know how much money you need to earn to cover expenses, bills, etc, it is
time to start brainstorming niches. It is definitely easier to sell items you know something about.

You will be faced with questions from prospective customers, and although you may include some research in your time, it is good to have a foundational knowledge going in so you do not get overwhelmed.

What are you interested in or passionate about? Clothes? Collectible cards or toys? Electronics? Remember, you can do as much or as little as you want, so perhaps choose a few if you can't narrow it down.

5.   Do not set it and forget it. There is a reason that items in stores are rotated
regularly. With the exception of certain basic products, stores want to turn over their products quickly.

Why?

To a potential customer, an item that does not seem to sell does not sell for reason. Maybe it's not popular, not useful, or not appealing. Bottom line is that you want to make sure your items are moving within the time limit you have set.

6.   To possibly contradict the last point, what is needed in the arena you are choosing? For
example, I knew I wanted to sell clothing. I purchased lots of [mostly] women's clothing in sizes ranging from extra small to 4x.

What I learned was that there is a great need in my area for varied women's clothing in sizes 1x-4x, as there is only 1 plus-size women's clothing store in my city.

It was very easy to sell those sizes, but the extra small and small items were extremely challenging to sell, and I actually (initially) took a small loss just trying to get rid of them and get a little bit of my money back.

7.	Social media etiquette. Here is a quick rundown of simple but IMPORTANT social
media dos and don'ts, if you want to use these mediums effectively for your reselling business.

1. DO dedicate pages on all social media streams to announce and promote your reselling business.

2. DON'T privately message people unless they initiate it.

3. DO post regularly, so that your presence doesn't become stale.

4. DON'T set up pre-written messages or responses that will make you appear cold and robotic.

5. DO engage your audience: answer questions, send out polls, and comment on their stuff, too.

6. DON'T fall into the follow-unfollow game. This is where you follow people so they will follow you back, then unfollow them so you have a higher following-to-follower ratio. People are getting wise to this and do not appreciate it.

7. DO share tips and tricks without expecting people to return the favour. Build that trust.

8. DON'T spam your audience with constant 'special buys.' It comes off as needy.

9. DO be honest AND stay within your scope of practice; if you promise unicorns and give your customers horses with paper mache horns you will quickly lose them.

8.   Over-deliver (packaging, note, etc). You can add a lot of perceived value with a little

effort. If you are selling new clothes, for example, and $30 for a top that you mention is of good quality and perfect for summer fun and THEN hand it to the customer in a plastic grocery store bag, you are possibly closing the door on future sales.

In the spring I bought a bunch of cheap but brightly coloured gift bags - pink, yellow, purple, green - for my clothing sales. The customers enjoyed getting a cute bag (that they can reuse!).

The best part? I worked the cost of the bags into the sales price so I didn't even have to pay out of pocket. The same can be said for thank-you notes.

People not only appreciate the effort, but it makes you more memorable. If you are memorable, people will return to you, recommend you, and more.

9.   Think about how you wish to stand out from your competition. Will you be focusing on
high quality items? Hard-to-find? Selling a high volume of inexpensive things? Something unique?

If you are selling leggings or wall decor or vintage games, what makes you memorable to people passing you by? When I worked at a market selling clothes, there was another vendor selling women's clothing. I stood out by having nicer racks and hangers, and a mannequin I would adorn with tunics and scarves.

Language can make a difference, too. I purchase all of my clothing for reselling online. When people inevitably asked: "Where do these come from?" I could respond as simply as "online."

But. Anyone can get clothing online. I chose my words carefully with the intention to continue to be honest, but with more impact: "I source each of my pieces online based on comfort and style. I try to stay trendy while keeping classic lines and colours so you can wear and enjoy them for years."

10.   Use feedback usefully... Feedback is an important tool that can help you to better your
business. The feedback can be direct or indirect; that is to say, it can come naturally from the customer or you can probe for it. I recommend working with both.

With direct feedback, you are asking people about their experience with you and what they would like to see you offer/other items they may be looking for. For example, when I posed this question to the women to whom I was selling clothes, they said they wanted to see items that are more unique-looking as well as more variety in size. I did both, and got more customers because of my adaptation.

With indirect feedback, you can take questions/concerns that customers may have and apply them. After getting a number of women asking me about types of material in the clothes I sold, I started including that information in the listing.

11.   ...But do not let criticism get to you. There is a marked difference between feedback and
         criticism. You can work hard and be honest and do the best you possibly can, and you will still encounter the occasional unsatisfied customer.

         Some people are just wired this way, or they're having a bad day, or..whatever! Frankly, it doesn't matter.

         What matters is that you do NOT take these less-than-perfect interactions to heart. I have had a few (and just a few) people who are outright angry with me for not delivering to them (though my ads say pick-up only), or not holding unpaid items for them (my ads say holds with payment only), or what have you. I do not hold it against these people, I just move on. On one or two occasions I have blocked access to me from someone who is trying to attack me, because I have neither the time nor patience to deal with such silliness.

         I didn't stew about it, I just moved on.

12.   That is to say, if there is an error from your end, it is important that you work to repair the
damage you have caused.

As much as you should expect reason and respect from your customers, they should get at least as much from you. I once mis-represented a size in my ad (an honest mistake but a mistake nonetheless) and when the lady came to pick up her item she was disappointed and I was embarrassed.

Time is important to people, and I had just wasted hers. So, after apologizing, I offered a similar item in the appropriate size to her for free, to make up for the mix-up.

She was satisfied with this, and ended up purchasing from me again, which made up for the $8 loss I had taken on from the free item. Saving the relationship was more valuable to me than a few dollars.

13.   Be resilient.

Reselling can be a dreamy, fun job but it has its tough moments, too. It ebbs and flows. This is true of all sales, on all scales. Perhaps you ordered a box of products and they arrive but are incorrect in some way, or damaged, and you have to go through the hassle of returning them. Or you have something in your personal life bleed into your work. Or you get into a work funk, burning yourself out.

It is normal. I promise. Weather the storm and you will come out on the other side.

I had a moment where I was SO frustrated, because I had purchased a bunch of jewelry for resale that I thought were quite pretty, but, for whatever reason, just didn't sell. I was annoyed with myself for not doing better research, I was mad at the customers who weren't taking advantage of my good prices, and I had money tied up that was staying tied up. I wanted to throw in the towel.

But I went back to my goals, realigned myself, and found a way to move them (selling in groups of three as a bundle deal). I also stopped checking my messages after 9pm.

When business is good, enjoy it thoroughly, and use that feeling during a down time to remind you that good times are coming again.

14.   Depending on the types of items you are reselling, it is important that you set a baseline
for percent profit so that you are actually making money from the items. For clothes, I aim for no less than 3x what I paid for them.

This allows me to regain my investment, and to buy two more of the same item (or other similarly-priced ones) so that I can grow exponentially.

I have also had good luck buying inexpensive but decent-quality jewelry items (especially necklaces and bracelets) and flipped them for a significant amount. The best I have done in my area is purchase a necklace for $1.29 and sold it for $25. That's a huge profit!

15.   Take the season into account. People are most likely to purchase items that are

seasonally appropriate. You will not sell as many winter boots, for example, in late spring as you will in early fall, even if your price is very competitive.

There are always outliers, of course, but it is still an important consideration. That being said, working within the seasons can do wonders for you when buying.

Winter boots go on sale in January because although the weather is cold, people are generally already equipped with what they need by that point. If you have the cash/space, buy off-season items to sit on for future sales.

16.   I am going to let you in on a secret: it is completely acceptable to miss out on a
        sale. Resellers can develop a habit of grabbing items because they are a good price - whether or not it actually makes sense for them to buy them.

Despite effective marketing about scarcity, there will ALWAYS be another deal in the future. Be smart about taking advantage of deals, rather than jumping on them just because they are there.

When I started, I purchased 150 dresses because they were $3 each. I figured I could sell them for $10 and make a tidy profit. Well. Based on the quality (noticeably poor) and sizes (most turned out to be extra small), I had a lot of difficulty actually moving them. I ended up selling them for roughly $4 each, which was completely not worth the time unpacking, folding, photographing, and listing them. Lesson learned. Just because it is a good price does not mean it is a good deal.

17.   Be prompt and polite. Buyers can be impatient, so if you take two days to answer a
question they have about your product, they have likely moved onto another seller/retailer by the time you finally get back to them.

And for goodness sake, use your manners. Use full sentences and proper grammar and spelling. All of those details may not have anything to do with the actual product, but it can make or break a sale. I know as a buyer, people expect to be respected, listened to, and have their questions answered.

One common question I receive with clothes is "is it true to size?" Instead of just typing "yes" and hitting send, I will take a minute to say "I will always be as accurate with sizing as I can be, to ensure you love the product. You are welcome to try it on before committing to buy. Does today or tomorrow work best for you?"

18.   Offer deals for repeat customers! After selling clothes for 3 months, I started getting
repeat buyers. This is great for a number of reasons: they are less likely to string you along or no-show, they are friendly and familiar with you, and - most importantly - they will talk about you to their friends!

There is a reason that you can get loyalty deals/cards/services with most large companies: it is easier to keep a customer than to try to get new ones. You don't have to destroy your profit to make them happy, but letting them know you are going to take a few extra dollars off because you appreciate their business goes a long, long way.

19.   Decide your parameters and be consistent. Do you plan to deliver items within your
city? Offer several shipping options? Have people come inside of your home? Though it may feel trivial, setting your parameters from the get-go will save you many headaches in the future.

It allows for simplistic conversation, keeps you consistent for all of your buyers, and keeps your stress to a minimum. For example, I work locally (I don't ship), I do not allow buyers in my house, I keep my phone alerts off so I can control when I receive messages, and I only do holds with payment.

I have encountered a few grumps who don't like my rules, but frankly you will encounter these people no matter what you do, so take care of yourself first.

20.   Reinvest your money! When you sell $100 worth of items for $400, it can be tempting to
celebrate with a little shopping spree. However, if you take that $300 profit and immediately reinvest it into more items to sell, you will grow much more quickly.

Depending on your needs, you can 'pay' yourself a percentage of what you earn from reselling. However, if you put that money back into your business you will be surprised at how quickly you can make a significant amount of cash.

Remember, you are currently existing on x amount of money already, any extra money wouldn't be there if you weren't reselling. Put that extra money back into your reselling business and trust me, you will be happy you did when you come on the other side with much more than that initial return.

21.   Utilize local marketing. I have had enormous success using Facebook
        Marketplace. Post an ad with pictures, and as people are scrolling through or searching for specific items, they can quickly let you know if they are interested.

        Another benefit of doing it this way is that people can search your name (or business name) in the search bar, and get access to all of your current ads. I can't tell you how many times someone has asked me about a shirt and ended up buying 3 or 4. Other resources include Kijiji, Craigslist, and even making up some flyers to post around in designated areas/store.

        Think about your own buying habits. If you want to sell refurbished guitars, where would you look if YOU were interested in shopping for one?

22.   Use markdowns creatively. Perhaps you want to do some reselling work but you don't
        have one specific niche.

        Be creative! Do you have a green thumb? Buy discounted plants and pots and ask garden centres if they have broken bags of soil they will sell to you for a steal. Make up a bunch of small tropical plant/flower pots. Handy with needle and thread? Scour the clearance racks at fabric/craft stores and make unique pillow covers or clothing articles.

        People love one-of-a-kind finds that no one else has. Trying a few different venues will also give you some insight into what works for you.

23.   Actually get started. This might seem obvious, but for many people, the biggest barrier
        to having a successful reselling business is actually DOING it. Maybe you have been thinking about it for days, years, or anywhere in between.

        While thinking about potential success can be a useful tool for staying motivated, if you don't ever take that leap then you cannot have the success you want and deserve. Take one step and the rest will follow. Buy some products, or post ads for items you have, or clean out the space in your closet or garage where you plan to store your items. Progress happens with action.

24.   Now, depending on what you plan to sell, I highly recommend choosing a reasonable
        turnover time to work with. This can vary greatly depending on the type of item you will be working with, your daily schedule/other obligations, etc.

        A good baseline (incidentally, the one I use) is 3 weeks. If I have an item I cannot sell within three weeks of listing, then I employ other strategies (keep reading below) to move it as quickly as possible and make a note to myself to not carry that one again.

        If you have something sitting in a listing for two long there are two main problems: 1 - people see it sitting there and assume it is not of value since it has not sold, and 2 - it is not making you any money.

        Setting a timeline goal also helps you to stay on track by letting you know that your items are desired and profitable, which will keep you motivated.

25.   Get organized. There are different aspects of a reselling job to stay on top of, and it is in
        your interest to develop your own organization system to keep these running efficiently.

> For example: I keep a spreadsheet, organized by month, that includes a list of every item I have. I include date purchased, date listed, a description, cost to me, projected earning, actual earning, and notes. This way, I know exactly what I have and how much money I am spending vs earning. The notes section allows me to look back to see if I should avoid certain things, or order them again.

> Being organized in your listings is important as well. I keep my descriptions concise and consistent. Eg, New with tags green women's sweater, size large, in perfect condition. Cute with leggings or jeans and functionally warm for cool fall mornings. Pick up only in x area.

> All of my listings look similar for 2 reasons: it allows me to write them up very quickly (time IS money!), and it gives my business a voice people recognize for future interactions and purchases.

> The last area of being organized is in the items themselves. I keep everything in one place together, on racks or laid out on a table adjacent to a rack. The last thing I want to do when getting ready for a buyer to stop by is to scramble to find what they want. And I keep bags there as well (reused plastic bags for used items and cute but inexpensive gift bags for new items).

26.   Short game vs Long Game - What is your plan with reselling? Is this a side-gig, a new
        job, something to get you through a lean period? Although your plans can change over time, it's useful to have an idea

in your mind of how long you plan to do this. That way, you can envision your future with it and make more specific plans.

Say, for example, that you want to make $5000 to pay off a credit card. That would be a short game. This way, you would plan how much you want to purchase based on how much money you want to make monthly so you can accomplish this goal. Or perhaps you want this to be a side gig to your regular job, with no defined end. This could give you extra spending or saving money.

Knowing this, you can decide how much you want to make your first month, then learn how to take what you learned from the month to be even more successful the following month, until you reach a point where you feel happy with your income and/or satisfied with your rate of growth.

27.   Photography - While you certainly do not have to be a professional photographer to

resell, it does pay to be able to take a decent photo. Images are protected by copyright, so it is important to take your own photos rather than using stock ones or the pictures from the company's website.

Most of us have phones with decent cameras, so there is no need to go out and spend your money on a fancy camera. There are five main tips I have learned and always used, that have served me very well:

Composition - As much as possible, try to take photos straight on, rather than from an angle. Ideally, your item should be in the centre of the image.

Lighting - The more light you have on an object, the better representation your customers will get for colour and texture. Always use natural light if possible, or white-based light bulbs if for some reason you can't use sunlight. For example, I take photos near a window with a white curtain, which diffuses the light. This allows the most natural light possible, without any harsh shadows or glare. Warm light bulbs tend to make your items look brassy, which is not visually appealing.

Multiples - Take photos of the front, back, closeup, opened and closed, whatever is necessary based on your item to showcase the whole thing. This allows customers to get a real view of what they are buying, and helps you to avoid having to go back and take additional pictures and inopportune times, which is not time-efficient.

Scaling - Depending on the item you have, setting something next to it for scale can be really valuable. A ruler or even a pen will work. It's a simple fix to help you to avoid having to answer the question "how big is it?" a hundred times. If you are selling clothing, a mannequin can be really helpful for length.

Background - Use. A. White. Background. 99% of the time, at least. It not only helps to bounce MORE light onto your object (remember above? Light = good), but it looks more clean, professional, and appealing to customers. I buy white poster board from the Dollar Store to accomplish this. Just try to get a matte one, not a shiny one. Your photos will thank you!

28.   Always grow - In sales we talk a lot about a 'growth mindset.' This is the concept of
avoiding stagnation, which leads to backsliding. Growth is often associated with making more money, but it actually comes in many different forms.

Growth can mean that you make more money from increasing your prices or your volume. Growth can also mean that you find a more efficient system for cataloguing or shipping, or that you learn some new service techniques, or that you expand into an additional revenue stream.

Growth is being a little better tomorrow than you are today, with intention and effort.

29.   An effective marketer knows one main thing: if you can link your product to an emotion
or event, it draws away attention from the price. This is why people are always having fun in advertisements, regardless is they are selling amusement park tickets or toothpaste.

You can do this on a smaller, more subtle scale in your ads. What is the difference between: "women's blue sweater size medium, $45" and "pumpkin picking chic - cozy navy sweater for outdoor fall activities, size medium, only $45"..? The first certainly tells you what you are getting, but the second paints a picture of how you will look in the sweater while you are doing something fun. The price is almost an afterthought.

30.   Be confident! Know your products and what they have to offer your
customers. Showcase that. Know your limits and boundaries and do not be afraid to stick to them.

Know that as you gain more and more success, you will be closer to accomplishing the goals you have set for yourself. If fear or doubt or insecurity creeps in, take some deep breaths and realign yourself. Putting yourself out there can be daunting - perhaps for some more than others - but if you come across as confident, you will be more prosperous.

If you come across as a nervous or indecisive person, you are more likely to have people try to bully cheaper prices from you, which will cut into the profits that YOU deserve. Confidence is important.

31.   Do a 1-question survey. Building on the feedback aspect, I highly recommend doing a
1-question survey with all of your customers. As sellers, sometimes we make the mistake of deciding what the public wants, rather than doing any work to see what the trends are.

A simple 1-question survey can accomplish that without annoying the customer: "What else would you like to see me sell in the future?" Now, you can word this a little differently to give it your voice if you prefer, but keep it simple and concise. What you are waiting to hear are common answers, or things you have not thought of yet.

Sometimes people will give you an answer that really will not end up being relevant to you. That is okay. But if you hear the same answer more than once, that is a good indicator that there is demand but no supply. That is where you fit in.

32.   Work an event - Depending on the types of items you are selling, hitting up a craft
show/market/pet show/car show/etc can be a great way to help to establish your name as a local seller.

Though many people use online buy-and-sell programs, there is still huge value in face-to-face time with customers. I worked at a local market for a few weekends and got to meet people who hadn't seen me online, and I set up a bunch of sales to coincide with my presence there to help me to look busy and popular. It worked like a charm.

Most of these venues charge a fixed rate for the day/weekend. Some places will supply tables, but it is always good to ask to see what you may or may not have access to. I was also delighted by the experience of working beside other vendors, who actually helped me by chatting with customers and saying complimentary things about my items (the favour of which I of course returned to their customers and wares).

33. Answer questions before they are asked. Writing a good description helps you to save time. You certainly do not want to be over-wordy, because then people don't read it. But you want to get all of the information that a potential customer might ask.

It is tedious and time-sucking to answer the same question individually, over and over. Of course this varies hugely depending on what you are selling. Electronics? Give model number and specs. Clothing? Include material composition. New in box, new without tags, this x that dimensions, where to pick up, etc.

Of course, you will still end up answering questions you have already answered in the description sometimes (that is simply a side-effect of working with people!), but overall it will save you time.

34.   Set time for admin. Whether you are running a website or selling from a local online
listing program, it can be easy to throw away precious time on administrative work.

Setting a fixed amount of time spent daily/weekly on admin ensures that you are dividing your time to all aspects of your endeavor, not just playing around with logos or spreadsheets.

I prefer doing my admin in the morning (15 minutes) and checking my emails/messages at allotted times throughout the day. Naturally you will spend more time getting everything started, but once you have your systems in place, trust me when I say you will not create fires by putting your phone down.

Having set times will also keep you more on task when you ARE working your admin duties, so that you are not sitting in front of a spreadsheet while scrolling your social media poison of choice.

35.   Give customers options. The thing about these options, though, is that they favour the
seller. When you provide options to a customer, they are inclined to pick one. You'll get the odd one here and there that challenges you, but most people will pick one.

For example:

Customer: I am interested in this item
You: Great, does today or tomorrow work best for you?
Customer: Tomorrow
You: Alright, morning, afternoon, or evening?

Customer: morning, around 10?
You: That works for me! Do you plan to pay with cash or e-transfer?
Customer: cash.
You: here is my address, see you tomorrow at 10! Have a lovely day.

This is a concise, positive transaction.

Sometimes you will encounter people who want your item, but cannot pick it up immediately. The only time I will allow a non-payment hold is with customers who have purchased from me before, who I can trust to honour their commitment.

Otherwise, I do holds with payment only. Your goal is to get products to people, but ultimately to make money for yourself. Do not feel bad about setting your requirements and sticking to them.

If it is Monday and someone says they will pick something up on Friday, so you hold it for them, you risk having them change their mind last minute, while you may turn away other buyers. So, again, we give them a choice:

Customer: I am interested in this item
You: Great, does today or tomorrow work best for you?
Customer: Actually, I can't pick it up until next weekend. Does Saturday work?
You: Saturdays are fine, but I on;y do holds with payment. Would you prefer to send an e-transfer now to hold the product? Otherwise I can send you a message on Saturday morning to let you know if it is still available.
Customer chooses.

This way, they have the option to hold, which is a potential future sale, but it allows you to still sell the item in the meantime if someone else wants it. If they are willing to etransfer to hold it, I would characterize them as a low-risk future buyer. If they don't hold it and ultimately move on without buying, YOU move on, too!

36.   Do a 'today only/this weekend only' sale. One technique commonly used in sales is
imposing a sense of urgency in potential customers. Phrases such as 'limited time' and 'while supplies last' help to drive the feeling of FOMO (fear of missing out) that can drive up sales.

This is an effective technique but one you want to use judiciously; you can easily over do it. I have done this when I had a small pile of items that simply weren't moving or generating much interest. I took them off of my listings for a week, then slashed the prices (still enough to make a small profit) and price them to move. This incentivised a number of people to scoop them up.

It is a great way to clearout older stock, reduce the quantity of an item you have, and just generally increase interest in your business.

37.   Mystery boxes. This is something you see most commonly on eBay, as opposed to
other selling venues. This is another way to gain intrigue, to move products, and add variety to your wares.

You place one or as many items you can in a nondescript box or bag, and advertise it as a mystery package! You give a general description so people at least sort of know what they're getting (sizes, approximate value, number of items) and offer it for a better price than they would get if they bought the items individually.

Not everyone will go for them, but some people cannot pass up on the allure. Just make sure that there is value to be had; that they aren't going to excitedly open their box and discover a bunch of ugly clothes that you were hoping to move quickly.

38.   Set goals. This ties back to short game vs long game, but is much more specific. Goals
help you to stay organized, stay focused, and measure whether or not you are having the success you wanted from the start.

There is a big difference between: "I want to resell as a side gig for some extra cash" and "I want to resell athletic footwear for men in my city and online through eBay to pay off my student loan. I am going to track my earnings and spending through a great app I found. I know where I can access great quality bulk shoes and have $500 to invest. Within 3 months I will triple my investment, and within a year I can pay off the remainder of my loan."

This is called SMART goal setting. Specific, Measureable, Attainable, Realistic, Timely.

It is a famously useful tool for not only identifying exactly what you want and how to get there, but also helps you to manage your expectations. Many people who start reselling will read stories about how they are earning a six-figure income within a year of starting. Although this may have happened to a few people, it is important to be realistic and manage your expectations.

This is not to say that your goal can't change over time. If you have never done any reselling before, there may be learning curves you weren't aware of. I had purchased a number of nice quality, very cute kids items that I was sure would sell immediately, especially since I got them for a good price and was able to offer competitive pricing on the market.

I ended up having an awful time trying to move them, and ended up just barely making my money back from that investment in order to actually move them. So I reset that part of my goals. To no longer include them.

Once you have your main, overarching goal, you can break it down into monthly and weekly goals, and then into daily tasks. This makes the whole process much less daunting.

39.   Friends/family discount. Chances are, your friends and family are going to be your
biggest fans. Let them know you appreciate their support by offering a little extra deal. That way, they can support you by shopping and spreading the word, while getting an exclusive discount (who doesn't love a discount?!).

I had a few family members who purchased items from me and while I was of course happy to hand them a deal, two additional bonuses happened. One, when I was visible at the market it made my booth look more busy. This adds perceived value to other customers, because people tend to want what others have.

Two, it boosted my online performance. Often when people are browsing online, they see something that they don't necessarily immediately buy, but come back to maybe a few times before hitting the 'purchase' button. There were a number of times when someone would reach out to ask if I 'still had that pretty grey tunic' to which I could reply: 'It already sold! Let me send you a few pictures of similar items you may like.'

40.   Fads - the double-edged sword. When a fad hits the scene, it hits hard. Everyone is
buying it, everyone is talking about it, and if you can get a good bulk deal it can certainly be tempting to jump on board.

But fads tend to wane as fast as they bloom, and being stuck with product that is suddenly unfashionable is very stressful.

I have sold a lot of women's tops, and the most popular colour is still black.

I recommend watching fads/trends, and proceeding with caution. This typically means buying an amount of product that you are very confident that you can sell quickly. With clothes, for example, I pay attention to trends but do not live by them.

I might buy a few extra things in a colour that is currently popular, but I make a point to try to move them quickly. There was a period of time recently where chevron pattern was extremely popular in both clothing and home decor, now it is out of style.

One way to make fads work for you, though, is to watch what countries who are leaders in the industry you plan to be marketing are doing. If I am looking for fashion cues, I turn my attention to Europe. Australia is a leader in the fitness world. North America has developed a bit of an obsession with the Danish concept of Hygge, which is all about comfort and coziness.

Watch the fads, participate if you want, but treat them like a warm day in November: enjoyable but fleeting.

41.   Do not bad mouth the competition. You will not be the only person selling what you are
        selling. You will be similar in some ways to your peers and different in others. Rather than focusing on who is doing 'better' and trying to ruin someone's business in order to promote yours, be a good sport and work with integrity.

        I worked with a wonderful team for three years as a personal trainer. We were all selling our services (which had similarities and differences) in the same area to the same population. We all had targets to reach and bills to pay. But we supported one another, celebrated all success, and it was a very positive, happy environment.

        At the end of the day you still want someone to buy your product instead of someone else's, yes. So think about how YOU can stand out, rise above, and become sought-after. Tell people why you believe your product is the best, and wish the other sellers the best of luck.

42.   Avoid manipulative closing techniques. There are so many useful selling techniques,
        and I recommend always continuing your education. But please be wary of being too 'salesy.' Customers these days are savvy to these techniques and they are quickly turned off by a seller using shrewd language to try to close a deal.

        One bad (and outdated) technique is offering a free item as a bonus if the client buys today. This does not come across as a good deal, but rather as a seller desperate to make a sale. Even if you ARE desperate, this will only backfire on you, as the person likely won't purchase at all and then VERY likely will not ever return.

Another mistake resellers can make is to chase a potential customer. Maybe someone reaches out to you about an item. You respond, and then there is nothing back from them. For days. You then reach back out 'are you still interested in this item?' which can seem desperate as well.

My rule is that I give a person 24 hours to respond, and then I delete the message and move on. Maybe they will come back and maybe not, but I am not spending my valuable time chasing down someone who clearly is not that interested.

The best advice I can give on closing is to be concise and authentic. The more you use your own voice (by that I mean written voice; how you sound in a text/email conversation), the more sincere you will appear to a customer. No one wants to be tricked into buying something, and manipulative closing techniques accomplish that and little more.

43.   Don't share your sources.

Remember when I said not to badmouth the competition? That still holds true, but it does not mean you have to create any competition for yourself. I have had people ask me where I get my goods, and I say - very honestly - 'I source them from a number of places online.' And I leave it at that.

Look, if someone is internet savvy enough, they can find the same places I have found. But I have worked hard to find these places, know what time of day or what day of the week to get the best deals, and how to negotiate with certain types of sellers. If someone else puts in the work to get there, then good for them! But unless I am being paid to consult that person, I will keep it to myself, thankyouverymuch.

And it is not being rude, I just want to protect my profits where I have the control to do so. For example, I enjoy making my own homemade soap. I do not sell it, I keep most of it and give some to family. I have no intention of selling it. But I would not ask the homemade soap lady at the market to tell me where she gets her supplies, because I do not want her to think I am trying to encroach on her business. If I want the best soap supply deals, I will research them myself.

44.   Develop a list of preferred customers.

There are more ways to honour repeat customers than offering discounts. I love working with repeat buyers because I know they are reliable, they know and are happy with my terms, and there is a camaraderie that builds.

You can keep a spreadsheet of a few details that will help you to go above and beyond for these customers. For example, I know that "Julie" (name changed of course) wears a size small, preferes tunic style and likes funky designs and patterns. "Marie" is 1x, she is quite tall and loves muted tones and lace detailing.

Knowing these details doesn't change my shopping patterns dramatically, but I do keep my eye out if I come across a piece I think they might like. Once it arrives, I will send them a message first before listing it, in case they want first grab. It's like a very light personal shopping job/experience. It makes them feel special and I have gotten referrals from both of them.

45.   Do a weekly check in with yourself. Along with having well-thought out goals outlined,
doing a regular check-in is going to help to both keep you accountable and quickly put the spotlight on any issues that may be quietly arising.

I like doing this weekly, but you can pick any interval that suits your schedule and personality. The main things I look for are:
Am I making the profit I had set as my goal?
Are there any issues I need to address?
What is going well?
What do I need to do differently?
Am I having my work-life balance needs met?

This is not a time-consuming task, but it should be integral that you refrain from skipping it.

46.   Get personal. One of the easiest ways to stand out from other resellers is to use the
best parts of your personality to your advantage. If you are an emphatic, bubbly person then that can be infectious. If you are, like me, more quiet but good with details, ask your customers personal questions that you can bring up again in future conversations ("Oh I remember you bought that sweater for your daughter! Did it look as pretty on her as you thought it would?"). People love to feel cared for.

Having handwritten tags and signs adds a cozy, intimate touch. Making friendly small talk at a booth helps people to feel connected to you. There are lots of ways to be personal, and lots of people who respond well to this style.

47.   Do not get personal. Clearly this is contradictory to the last point, but being

affectionately called 'The Robot' by a few loved ones, I know from experience that being too personal can completely turn a customer away. Read your audience. Some people will be more up for chatter, others will give you polite, concise responses and go back to their browsing. Let them. Be still and allow them to shop on their own terms.

Another part of this is that sometimes people will try to get more out of you than you are willing to give by offering sad stories about their day or their life. True or not, if you are all sympathy and no logic, you are the one who will lose on your business.

I had a lady who told me I "should do a kind thing for once" by delivering a top to her (I never deliver). I told her while I am a kind person, I turn down delivery requests regularly and that it would not be fair for me to give her special treatment.

Be kind but be assertive and watch the body language cues to decide how to work with an individual person.

48.   Step outside your comfort zone. I know, this is an old and slightly boring sentiment, but I
          really feel it works here.

Along with the niche you are comfortable with selling, you should try to sell something that you don't know as much about. This is a solid way to boost your brain creatively.

When you do not know something, you are inclined to research it. You will then want to market it in a certain way, based on the information you have gathered or the niche group you know you will be catering to.

I decided to sell some Nordic jewelry because there were a few popular Hollywood movies/shows that featured the culture (or a fictional culture rooted in it), and because Nordic-style kitchenware was gaining popularity.

I spent maybe an hour reading about the basic concepts and some symbols and low-and-behold, I sold out almost immediately of the pieces I had. This small (but intense) niche group in my area was so excited to get their hands on some items that represented the culture they were interested in. And I learned how to cater to them.

Stepping outside your comfort zone doesn't have to be dramatic, but it can really pay off and open your options further. The possibilities are endless.

49.   Get some air. You can take this advice literally and figuratively, and I recommend that
         you do both.

If you are feeling frustrated or overwhelmed, step away from your products and listings. The human brain is really proficient at processing information while otherwise occupied. If you are stuck or unhappy, get some exercise, do some rage cleaning, sit with a book, do whatever it is that is going to distract you and make you feel good. This way, when you come back to the task at hand, you are working with a fresh and useful mind, instead of a muddled one.

Getting air can also mean stepping away from your own business and checking out what other people are doing in theirs. I am by no means encouraging you to steal specific ideas, but use it as a source of education and inspiration to make yours better when you feel stuck.

50.   Never stop learning. Set aside some time each week or month to read an article or blog
        post about sales, reselling, detailed information about the types of products you sell, etc. Being more educated in this field will never disappoint you, and will inevitably help you to stay ahead as our consumer nations are always growing and evolving.

        What worked for people in sales 30 years ago is now outdated. New data, studies, and social media pressures are coming out every day. The more focused you are on staying ahead of the curve, the more you will continue to shine and not get left in the dust.

51.   Work in numbers, not emotion. This is my absolute best advice when it comes to
        sales. It can be so easy to tie thoughts and feelings to your success, but, at the end of the day, it all comes down to data.

        The success you gain from sales does not have anything to do with luck, fate, or the will of the universe. It comes from logistics, which you can clearly see in the Measurable aspect of your SMART goal setting.

        If you set a goal of earning $500/month in reselling sales, and you fall short, the worst thing you can do is to explain it away without addressing where the bleeding is. Do not blame outside influences (time of year, weather, I had the flu, customer had the flu, blah blah) but rather look at your process and methods to determine what you can do TODAY to improve your success.

        Your job in selling your items is to make the allure of the products more than any barriers the customer might encounter. If a potential customer ends up not buying because 'something came up,' then you did not do your job as a seller to make the product so necessary in their life that they will go out of their way to get it.

If your sales stagnate or - worse - start sliding backward, go back and reassess. Ask yourself some questions:
        What did you do in the past that helped you to achieve success?
        Are your photos working? Your descriptions?
        What barriers (time, money, distance) are customers portraying to you that you need to overcome?
        Are my goals realistic for this time?
        What article/book can I read that might educate me and make me better?

Do not make excuses, and do not accept failure. You are the only one controlling your ship, and it is up to you to get it where it needs to go.

It is time to wrap up, and send you on your way to start your reselling business. I trust you have read all of the points thoroughly and know where your individual strengths and weaknesses may lie, to give you an idea of where to target your vision. Reselling is a rewarding, lucrative opportunity to make money selling products you know and believe in. I feel confident that you can now avoid some of the errors that I have made, and encounter success comparable (or better!) to my own. Stay focused, be resilient, and be a little better each day.

www.ingramcontent.com/pod-product-compliance
Lightning Source LLC
Chambersburg PA
CBHW030548220526
45463CB00007B/3029